HIDE-AND-SEEK

with
DOT AND FRIENDS

By Anastasia Walton

Dot and her friends are playing hide-and-seek.

Dot is it!

1, 2, 3, 4, 5,

HERE I COME!

Dot hears a HONK somewhere close.

Can you find Goldie the Goose?

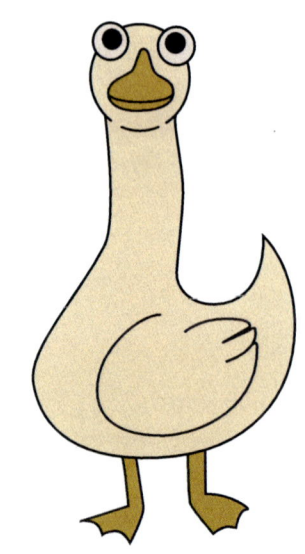

Found you, Goldie!

Goldie is found.

Four more friends to find!

One of their friends lives under water.

Can you find Serena the Sea Serpent?

Serena is found.

Three more friends to find!

Someone small could hide at the campsite.

Can you find Felix the Phoenix?

Felix is found.

Two more friends to find!

Maybe one of their friends is hiding far away.

Can you find Dreamer the Dragon?

We found you, Dreamer!

Dreamer is found.

One more friend to find!

The horses are having a hat party.

Can you find Ube the Unicorn?

Ube is found.

No more friends to find!

Let's play again!

Goldie is it, so everyone else will go hide.

7, 8, 9, 10, READY OR NOT, HERE I COME!

Can you find all of Goldie's friends?

Made in the USA
Coppell, TX
10 September 2023